THE UPDATED DANUBE RIVER CRUISE TRAVEL GUIDE

(A Comprehensive Guide to an Unforgettable River Cruise Adventure for 2023 -2024)

BY

FLORY ADAMS

Contents

.

STORY OF A TRAVELLER

Embarking on a journey of enchantment, my husband and I embarked on a cruise that swept us from the heart of Bavaria to the captivating embrace of Budapest, all along the illustrious Danube. Our voyage was no ordinary one – it was a winter escapade that unfolded amidst the timeless charm of traditional Christmas Markets. As we navigated this ethereal route, the markets unfurled before us, nestled beneath the watchful gaze of castles that seemed to guard centuries of stories, and cathedrals that whispered of devotion and history.

Amidst the glistening snow and the promise of festive cheer, we found ourselves enveloped in the magic of these markets. Each one carried a unique essence, an echo of the culture that thrived within its confines. And as we wandered through the stalls, pausing to savor local delights and admire handcrafted treasures, we felt a kinship with the souls who had walked these paths before us, seeking joy and celebration.

Guiding us through this journey were the remarkable individuals who wore the mantle of guides. With an unparalleled passion for the arts and culture of the destinations we traversed, they transformed each stop into a living tableau of history and heritage. They shared tales that wove the past into the present, breathing life into every cobblestone and echoing chamber. Through their narratives, the castles, cathedrals, and charming streets became more than just landmarks – they became living embodiments of the stories that had shaped the Danube's shores.

As we ventured from one destination to another, we found ourselves immersed in a tapestry of experiences. From the warmth of Bavaria to the elegance of Vienna and the enigmatic allure of Budapest, the Danube carried us through a symphony of emotions. We marveled at the twinkling lights that danced upon the river's surface, and we reveled in the camaraderie of fellow travelers, each of whom added a unique hue to the canvas of our journey.

And so, as the winter days turned to nights and the melodies of Christmas echoed in the air, we knew that this voyage was more than just a cruise – it was an odyssey of the heart and soul. It was a journey that whispered of the beauty of tradition, the resilience of culture, and the unbreakable thread that binds us all – the thread of humanity seeking connection and celebration. And as we retraced our steps, from Bavaria's embrace to Budapest's allure, we carried with us not just the memories of the journey, but the essence of the Danube itself – a river that flows not just with water, but with stories, dreams, and the promise of discovery.

INTRODUCTION

Exploring the Danube - A Beginner's Guide to River Cruising Adventures

Welcome to the enchanting world of Danube River cruising, where history, culture, and natural beauty come together to create an unforgettable journey. Whether you're a seasoned traveler or embarking on your very first adventure, this guide is your gateway to unlocking the secrets of one of Europe's most iconic waterways.

The Danube River weaves through the heart of Europe, connecting captivating cities, charming villages, and breathtaking landscapes. As you embark on this cruise, you'll be treated to a unique blend of experiences that range from exploring historic castles to immersing yourself in the vibrant cultures of Vienna, Budapest, and beyond. This guide has been crafted to serve as your compass, helping you navigate every aspect of your river cruising experience.

Did you know that the Danube River flows through ten countries, making it a true crossroads of cultures and traditions? From the medieval castles that dot its banks to the vibrant cities that line its shores, every bend of the Danube holds a story waiting to be discovered. This travel guide is your key to unlocking the wonders of Danube River cruising, providing you with not only essential itineraries but also a wealth of fascinating insights.

A Journey Through Time: The History of Danube River Cruises

Embarking on a Danube River cruise is more than just a contemporary travel experience – it's a voyage through centuries of history, culture, and human interaction. As you navigate the waters of the Danube, you are following in the wake of empires, traders, artists, and explorers who have left their mark on this iconic European waterway. From the ancient routes of the Romans to the modern luxury cruise ships of today, the history of the Danube River is a captivating narrative that unfolds with every bend and curve.

The story of the Danube River begins in antiquity. As one of Europe's longest and most significant rivers, it served as a natural pathway for civilizations to connect and thrive. In the time of the Roman Empire, the Danube played a vital role in trade and communication. The Romans recognized its strategic importance and established settlements and fortifications along its banks to facilitate the movement of goods and people.

As the Middle Ages dawned, the Danube continued to be a lifeline of commerce. It connected major cities, enabling the exchange of goods, ideas, and cultures. The river's strategic value led to the establishment of trading posts and fortresses that guarded its passages. The Danube's flow became intertwined with the historical tapestry of Europe, shaping the destinies of nations and shaping the course of events.

The concept of leisurely cruising along the Danube began to take shape in the 19th century. The introduction of steam-powered ships revolutionized river travel, making it more comfortable and accessible. The Danube's picturesque landscapes and historic cities captured the imagination of travelers seeking to explore the cultural treasures of Europe. Pleasure cruises along the river became a fashionable pursuit, allowing the well-to-do to indulge in luxury while taking in the sights.

The 20th century posed challenges to the progression of river travel. World Wars and political upheavals disrupted the stability of the region, impacting tourism along the Danube. Despite these setbacks, the post-World War II era witnessed a renewed interest in exploring the historic cities and landscapes along the river. Governments and cruise operators worked to modernize and rebuild river tourism infrastructure, leading to the renaissance of the Danube River cruise industry.

Today's Danube River cruises blend the comforts of modern luxury with a deep respect for the historical significance of the regions visited. The vessels that ply the Danube offer a level of elegance and sophistication that is a far cry from the boats of centuries past. Travelers now have the opportunity to experience the beauty and cultural heritage of cities like Vienna, Budapest, and Bratislava in unprecedented comfort.

As you sail along the Danube's meandering course, you are traversing not only its waters but also the pages of history. The castles that grace its banks, the cathedrals that dominate the skyline, and the villages that have stood for centuries are all part of the narrative that unfolds around you. With each passing day, you're following in the wake of emperors, artists, and thinkers who were inspired by the Danube's beauty and majesty.

Cruising the Danube also offers a culinary exploration of the regions it traverses. The river's history has contributed to the diverse culinary traditions found along its course. From the hearty dishes of Hungary to the delicate pastries of Austria, each meal tells a story of the influences that have shaped the region's cuisine over time.

As you embark on your Danube River cruise, you are becoming a part of this storied history. Your experiences, interactions, and memories become threads in the tapestry of the Danube's narrative. Whether you're exploring historic landmarks, savoring local flavors, or engaging with the people you meet, you're contributing to the ongoing legacy of the river.

As you journey through time along the Danube's currents, you're embracing the essence of exploration that has defined the river for centuries. From the ancient Romans to the modern-day traveler, the allure of the Danube remains timeless. As you chart your course through its waters, you're not only discovering the past but also creating a chapter of your own in the ongoing history of the Danube River.

A Journey of Discovery: The Itineraries Await

Imagine sailing from the romantic streets of Budapest, known as the "Pearl of the Danube," to the opulent palaces of Vienna, where the melodies of Mozart and Strauss still resonate in the air. Or perhaps you're drawn to the hidden gems of the Wachau Valley, a UNESCO World Heritage Site, where terraced vineyards meet charming villages like Dürnstein and Melk with its magnificent abbey. From the artistic flair of Linz to the historic allure of Bratislava, your Danube River cruise promises an array of experiences that cater to every traveler's passion.

Unveiling the Danube's Secrets: Historical Tidbits and Local Insights

Beyond the iconic sights, the Danube's waters hold tales of empires rising and falling, of revolutions and renaissances. Learn about the Habsburg dynasty's influence on the region, the strategic importance of the Danube during various periods, and the modern-day reflections of its storied past. Engage with the local cultures through immersive excursions that allow you to savor authentic cuisine, interact with artisans, and witness traditions that have been preserved for generations.

Planning Your Perfect Cruise: Tailoring Your Experience

Choosing the ideal Danube River cruise involves more than just selecting a departure date. Discover the nuances of cruise lines, vessel types, and on-board amenities that cater to your preferences. Whether you seek a romantic getaway, an enriching cultural exploration, or a festive holiday market experience, we'll guide you in finding the cruise that aligns with your dreams.

Prepare to be swept away by the elegance and diversity of the Danube River, as you embark on a journey that promises not just a vacation, but a transformational adventure.

Why Choose a River Cruise on the Danube?

Unlike ocean cruises, which often focus on large, bustling ports, a Danube River cruise offers an intimate and immersive journey. Imagine waking up each morning to the gentle lapping of water against the ship's hull, with a new destination to explore right at your doorstep. River cruises grant you access to picturesque landscapes that remain hidden from larger vessels, allowing you to get up close and personal with the region's hidden treasures.

For those seeking a river cruise brimming with diversity, the Danube stands out as an exceptional choice. A glance at the map reveals the Danube River's course slicing through the very heart of Europe, meandering from the Black Forest in the west to the Black Sea in the east. Remarkably, this river traverses a total of 10 countries, including Austria, Hungary, Serbia, and Slovakia – a feat unmatched by any other river worldwide. Along its banks, a showcase of European architectural brilliance unfolds, from the neo-Gothic spires of the Hungarian Parliament Building to the majestic towers of Regensburg Cathedral. Contemporary marvels also grace the landscape, such as Linz's sleek Ars Electronica Center and the modern Lentos Art Museum. Embarking on a week-long Danube River cruise transports you from Budapest's famed thermal baths to Bratislava's vibrant bars. You can immerse yourself in Vienna's rich musical heritage at its renowned coffeehouses and opera venues, all while discovering the echoes of Mozart. Moreover, the opportunity arises to explore ancient wine towns nestled in Austria's picturesque Wachau Valley, including Durnstein and Melk. Alternatively, you can venture further eastward, cruising past Serbia's awe-inspiring Iron Gates – a gorge replete with breathtaking vistas. For a more expansive experience, consider combining your Danube cruise with a journey along the Main on our comprehensive two-week European Icons itinerary. This extended route grants you the privilege of encountering cities like Amsterdam and Cologne, along with charming wine-growing towns such as Bamberg and Rudesheim. The journey culminates with the continuation to Vienna, Bratislava, and Budapest, completing an extraordinary odyssey through Europe's captivating tapestry.

So, whether you're a history enthusiast, a food lover, an avid photographer, or simply a curious traveler seeking a unique experience, this guide is tailored to your interests. We invite you to dive into the chapters ahead, each of which holds a piece of the Danube's rich tapestry, waiting to be discovered and woven into the story of your own journey.

Get ready to set sail on the Danube, where every bend of the river reveals a new chapter in your exploration. Your adventure starts now!

CHAPTER TWO:

Embarking on the Danube River Cruise Adventure

The Danube River, often referred to as "Europe's Queen of Rivers," meanders through a tapestry of landscapes, cultures, and history. This chapter will be your gateway to understanding the essentials of planning and experiencing an unforgettable Danube River cruise, offering insights into the river's significance, the diverse cruise itineraries, the ideal times to set sail, and the intricacies of planning and booking your journey.

Navigating the Legendary Danube River

The Danube's journey is a captivating one, spanning approximately 2,850 kilometers (1,770 miles) and passing through ten countries: Germany, Austria, Slovakia, Hungary, Croatia, Serbia, Bulgaria, Romania, Moldova, and Ukraine. This river has been a lifeline for trade, transportation, and cultural exchange for centuries, bearing witness to the rise and fall of empires, the birth of art and music, and the flow of human stories.

The river's diverse landscapes range from the lush vineyards of Austria's Wachau Valley to the rugged gorges of the Iron Gates in Serbia. Its serene bends reveal fairy-tale castles, ancient monasteries, and charming villages that seem to have been plucked from the pages of history. As you embark on your cruise, each destination will unveil a piece of the Danube's multifaceted character.

Selecting the Perfect Cruise Itinerary in 2023, 2024 and beyond

Choosing the right cruise itinerary is akin to selecting a tailored suit – it should reflect your personal style and interests. Do you long to explore the imperial grandeur of Vienna or to indulge in Budapest's vibrant cultural scene? Perhaps you're drawn to the medieval charm of Regensburg or the serenity of the Danube Delta as it meets the Black Sea. This chapter will guide you through the array of options, helping you align your desires with the experiences that each itinerary promises.

Here are a selection of leading Danube River tours and cruises set for 2024:

Danube Waltz with Viking River Cruises:

Embark on an 8-day voyage from Budapest to Vienna, encompassing some of the Danube's most historic and picturesque cities such as Bratislava, Melk, and Wachau. Travelers can partake in included activities such as a tour of the Hungarian Parliament Building, a serene Danube River cruise, and a delightful wine tasting experience in the Wachau Valley.

Grand Danube Cruise with AmaWaterways:

This 12-day expedition from Budapest to Amsterdam traverses nine countries and halts at iconic urban destinations like Vienna, Budapest, and Prague. Guests can choose from an array of inclusive excursions, including a guided stroll through Budapest, a visit to the Auschwitz-

Birkenau Memorial and Museum, and a leisurely boat ride along Prague's Charles Bridge.

Splendors of Europe with Scenic Cruises:

Unveil the Upper Danube's treasures during an 11-day escapade from Amsterdam to Budapest, embracing highlights like the Wachau Valley, Melk Abbey, and the Danube Bend. Travelers are treated to included activities such as an exploration of Vienna's Hofburg Palace, a serene Danube River voyage, and an indulgent wine-tasting event in the Wachau Valley.

Christmas Markets on the Danube with Avalon Waterways:

Embrace the festive spirit during a 7-day yuletide cruise from Budapest to Vienna. Delight in the enchanting Christmas markets in each city, and take advantage of a selection of inclusive excursions, from touring the Hungarian Parliament Building to a serene Danube River sojourn and relishing a traditional Hungarian Christmas feast. immersing yourself in the charm and history of towns like Bratislava, Melk, and Dürnstein. Participate in included activities, such as a guided walking tour of Budapest, an exploration of the majestic Melk Abbey, and a tranquil boat ride along the Danube River.

Discover the Charms of Southeast Europe

Step aboard the Amamagna for an enchanting 8-day journey tracing the Danube River's course. Setting sail from Budapest, embark on an intimate voyage that introduces you to quaint villages, historical marvels, and the lavish comforts of the ship. Immerse yourself in the unique allure of Southeast Europe as you traverse from Bulgaria to Serbia, navigating the famed "Iron Gates" of the Danube. Savor the region's delectable wines against the backdrop of serene river scenes. With choices for wine-tasting ventures, explorations of historic landmarks, and a variety of expert-guided tours, this cruise promises a fulfilling experience tailored to all preferences.

Exploring Eastern Europe's Finest: From Budapest to Bucharest

Embark on a captivating journey tracing the footsteps of historical figures, traversing Hungary, Serbia, Croatia, Romania, and Bulgaria. Experience the rich tapestry of cultures as you venture from the magnificent city of Budapest to the vibrant Bucharest. This remarkable 10-day cruise aboard the S.S. Beatrice promises a deep immersion into the resurgent Eastern European nations.

Marvel at the grandeur of Hungary's Parliament Building as it graces the Budapest skyline, evoking the legacies of crusaders, monarchs, and conquerors. Engage in convivial conversations over shared meals with local farmers in Croatia and enthusiastic residents in Bulgaria, forging connections that transcend borders.

On this transformative voyage, embrace the history, culture, and camaraderie that characterize the revitalized nations of Eastern Europe.

Journey of the Black Sea: Budapest - Bucharest

Embark on an expedition through the captivating epochs of history, delving into the enchanting Eastern European tapestry during a 9-day river cruise on the esteemed Scenic Pearl. Your odyssey commences in Budapest, unfurling through Kalocsa, Osijek, and Belgrade. Revel in serene moments as you traverse the iconic Iron Gates, a breathtaking natural boundary between Romania and Serbia. Delve into Bulgarian life as you uncover the charms of Svishtov, Rousse, Silistra, and Giurgiu before concluding in Bucharest, where glimpses of its communist past await.

Danube's Treasures

Anticipate a journey replete with unexpected delights as you traverse the captivating realm of this stunning region. Embark on a lavish 5-star river cruise aboard the Scenic Opal, where every facet of this itinerary promises to captivate and astonish. Commence your odyssey in Nuremberg, a city steeped in history both ancient and contemporary; delve into its old town and absorb its multifaceted role in the annals of time. Immerse yourself in the cultural heart of Vienna, a city adorned with resplendent architecture and steeped in a rich musical heritage. Culminate your exploits in Budapest, a European gem of unparalleled beauty, boasting myriad avenues for exploration. All this and more awaits you, all within the lap of luxury aboard your opulent river vessel.

A Journey along the Enchanting Danube

Embark on an adventure through captivating cities, commencing with a magical 3-night sojourn in the fairytale realm of Prague. This is followed by an 8-day voyage along the timeless Danube River, tracing the route from Vilshofen to Budapest. Immerse yourself in the legacy of a 2,000-year-old city, marvel at Europe's grandest pipe organ, indulge in local wines amidst the breathtaking Wachau Valley, and let your senses be entranced by the enduring beauty and profound history of both Vienna and Budapest.

Danube Dreams Unveiled (Eastbound)

Embark on a remarkable voyage with a prelude of two nights in Prague, where a series of tours unveils its most iconic treasures. Immerse yourself in guided sightseeing within Regensburg, encompassing landmarks like the Old Town Hall, Porta Pretoria, and opulent mansions adorned with lofty towers, emblematic of their early owners' affluence. Transition to Deggendorf, heralding the commencement of your river cruise adventure. Traverse the city of Passau in the company of a local guide. Revel in the splendid vistas as your river cruise meanders through the enchanting Wachau Valley, renowned for its picturesque vineyards. The journey advances to Dürnstein, where a wine immersion awaits, and then onwards to Vienna and Bratislava, both featured in guided tours. Conclude your odyssey by disembarking in Budapest, enriched by the myriad experiences along the Danube's captivating path.

Majestic Danube Exploration Vilshofen to Budapest

Set against a backdrop of rolling hills, verdant vineyards, and ancient castles, the Danube River has entranced musicians, artists, and poets across the ages. Embark on an unforgettable 7-night journey from Vilshofen to Budapest, unveiling legendary destinations along the way. Immerse yourself in a city with a two-millennia history, relish the flavors of Wachau Valley wines, and encounter the enduring allure and captivating history of Vienna and Budapest.

Danube & Prague Expedition- Vienna to Prague

Embark on an immersive journey along the Danube River, uncovering the enchanting outdoors and unique encounters that grace the cities of fabled tales. Prague, a city of wonders, boasts the colossal Hradčany Castle, renowned as the world's largest and most extraordinary, as well as an Old Jewish Quarter steeped in centuries of both adversity and jubilation. Traverse the ancient walled city and experience the allure of Nuremberg's captivating castles through the Nuremberg Panoramic City Tour. Confront and delve into the complex and haunting history of the region, resonating with the haunting echoes of the infamous Nazi documentation centers and party rally grounds.

In the historic heart of Vienna, be captivated by a tapestry of exquisite cuisine, wines, art, and outdoor adventures, all woven into the search for fresh inspiration along the graceful course of the Danube.

The Best Time to Embark on Your Adventure

The timing of your Danube River cruise can significantly influence your experience. Spring, from April to early June, ushers in mild weather, blooming landscapes, and festive events like the May wine festivals. Summer, from June to August, offers warmer temperatures, longer days, and a lively atmosphere. Fall, from September to October, graces the region with crisp air and vibrant foliage, along with harvest festivals and markets.

Cultural festivals and events pepper the calendar throughout the year, offering opportunities to engage with local traditions and celebrations. Understanding the seasonal rhythms will help you choose when to embark on your journey based on your preferences and interests

- The period of March, April, and May brings a mix of pleasantness and variability. While spring in Europe can be characterized by rain and lingering coldness, it's advisable to dress in layers. The arrival of spring can also bring about the melting of snow in the mountains, potentially causing flooding along the Danube river. When water levels rise significantly, it can hinder the passage of riverboats under narrow bridges and through specific locks. When such situations arise, river cruise companies frequently use buses to transport passengers to various destinations.
- Autumn Presents an Excellent Opportunity to Experience the Beauty of the Danube River

The nights become shorter, and temperatures decrease, but autumn provides an optimal chance to explore. Water levels have generally stabilized, the crowds have dispersed, fares are more affordable, and a pleasant coolness fills the air. It's advisable to bring layers for comfort.

- Late November and December Offer an Ideal Timing for Discovering Europe's Christmas Markets

Cruising along the Danube during this period of the year, with its Christmas Markets in various cities, creates a truly enchanting experience. Although the weather might be chilly, the presence of gluhwein and festive spirit keeps you warm. Shoppers will find it delightful. Make sure to bring winter coats, hats, gloves, and other items to stay cozy, as snowfall is a possibility.

Planning and Booking Your Dream Cruise

Turning your dream of a Danube River cruise into reality involves practical steps and careful consideration. Selecting the right cruise line, cabin type, and optional excursions can greatly enhance your experience. Booking early ensures availability and allows you to secure the best deals. Navigating the logistics of flights, transfers, and pre- or post-cruise extensions demands thoughtful planning, and our guide is here to provide you with expert advice and insights.

With the anticipation building, it's time to prepare for the adventure that awaits. From the river's origins in Germany's Black Forest to its final embrace with the Black Sea, the Danube promises an expedition into Europe's heart and soul. As you embark on this journey, remember that the river's currents carry not only water but the stories of countless civilizations – stories you're about to become a part of.

Here are some steps to remember while you plan a Danube River cruise:

1. Set a budget: Danube River cruises can range in price from a few thousand dollars to over ten thousand dollars per person, depending on the length of the cruise, the level of luxury, and the time of year. It's important to set a budget early on in the planning process so that you don't overspend.

2. Choose an itinerary: There are many different Danube River cruise itineraries to choose from, so it's important to choose one that fits your interests and budget. If you're interested in history and culture, you might want to choose a cruise that visits major cities like Vienna, Budapest, and Prague. If you're looking for a more relaxing cruise, you might want to choose a cruise that focuses on smaller towns and villages.

3. Research different cruise lines: There are many different Danube River cruise lines to choose from, each with its own unique style and amenities. Some of the most popular cruise lines include Viking River Cruises, AmaWaterways, Scenic Cruises, and Avalon Waterways. It's important to research different cruise lines to find one that's a good fit for you.

4. Consider the time of year: The best time to go on a Danube River cruise is during the summer months (June to August) or the fall months (September to

October). The weather is mild during these times, and there are fewer crowds.

5. Book your cruise early: Danube River cruises can sell out quickly, especially during peak season. It's important to book your cruise early to avoid disappointment.

6. Get travel insurance: Travel insurance can help protect you in case of unexpected events, such as flight cancellations, medical emergencies, or lost luggage. It's a good idea to get travel insurance for any trip, but it's especially important for a Danube River cruise since it can be expensive to cancel or change your plans.

7. Pack your bags: Be sure to pack comfortable shoes for walking, sunscreen, a hat, and sunglasses. You may also want to pack a raincoat or umbrella, as the weather can be unpredictable in Europe.

8. Learn some basic phrases in German: German is the most widely spoken language in the countries along the Danube River. It's helpful to learn some basic phrases in German so that you can communicate with locals and ask for directions.

9. Be flexible: Things don't always go according to plan on a cruise, so it's important to be flexible. Be prepared for delays, cancellations, and other unexpected events.

10. Have fun! A Danube River cruise is a great way to see some of the most beautiful and historic cities in Europe. Relax, enjoy the scenery, and make some new memories.

CHAPTER THREE

Destinations Along the Danube - Unveiling a Tapestry of History and Culture

Welcome to a chapter that invites you to step into a world where history is etched into every cobblestone, where architectural marvels bear witness to the passage of time, and where the cultures of Europe converge in a harmonious symphony of experiences. In this voyage through the destinations along the Danube, we will delve into the intricacies of each city, village, and hidden gem that lines the river's banks, revealing the stories that have shaped the region's past and continue to inspire its present.

The Enchanting Cities of Vienna, Budapest, and Prague: Imperial Opulence and Cultural Grandeur

The journey begins with Vienna, a city that encapsulates the spirit of an empire at its zenith. As you step onto the historic streets, you'll be swept into a world where the opulence of palaces meets the sophistication of coffeehouses. The Hofburg Palace, once home to the Habsburgs, emanates an air of regal elegance. Dive into the world of music at the Vienna State Opera, where the melodies of Mozart, Strauss, and Beethoven resound through the ages.

Vienna: A Majestic Jewel on the Danube's Crown
As your Danube River cruise meanders through the heart of Europe, there's one city that stands as a testament to the region's imperial past and artistic legacy – Vienna. Nestled

along the banks of the Danube, this Austrian capital exudes an air of sophistication and grandeur that captivates every traveler fortunate enough to visit its storied streets.

A Musical Capital: Waltzing Through Vienna's Melodies
Vienna's connection to music is as intrinsic as the Danube's flow itself. This city has been a muse to some of history's greatest composers, from Mozart to Beethoven, Haydn to Strauss. As your ship docks in Vienna, the melodies of classical compositions seem to echo through the air, inviting you to follow in the footsteps of these musical maestros.

The Vienna State Opera, an architectural marvel, is not merely a venue; it's a hallowed ground where the world's finest performances take center stage. Attending a live opera or ballet here is akin to stepping into a realm of artistry and emotion, where the acoustics transport you to another dimension.

Imperial Splendor: Palaces, Parks, and Pastimes
Vienna's imperial history is palpable as you explore its opulent palaces and manicured parks. The Schönbrunn Palace, a UNESCO World Heritage Site, is a masterpiece of Baroque architecture that once served as the summer residence of the Habsburgs. Stroll through its lavishly adorned rooms, marvel at the grandeur of the Hall of Mirrors, and wander through the palace's sprawling gardens, where meticulously manicured hedges and fountains create an oasis of tranquility.

The Hofburg Palace, another jewel in Vienna's crown, offers insight into the lives of Austria's ruling dynasties. From the

Imperial Apartments to the Sisi Museum, this complex is a living testament to the imperial lifestyle, complete with stories of emperors, empresses, and the intricate web of courtly intrigue.

Café Culture and Culinary Delights

Vienna's café culture is as much a part of its identity as its historical landmarks. The city's coffeehouses are not mere eateries; they're cultural institutions where locals and travelers alike gather to savor aromatic brews and engage in intellectual discussions. Café Central, one of Vienna's most iconic coffeehouses, has hosted luminaries like Freud and Trotsky, and stepping into its ornate interiors is like stepping back in time.

As you indulge in Vienna's culinary scene, don't miss out on its signature dishes. From the delightful Sachertorte – a decadent chocolate cake – to the savory Wiener Schnitzel, the city's gastronomy is a celebration of flavors that mirror its diverse cultural heritage.

Exploring Vienna on Your Danube Cruise

Vienna's allure is woven into the very fabric of the Danube's journey. As you step ashore, you'll be greeted by a city that seamlessly marries its past with its present. Whether you're marveling at the intricate architecture of St. Stephen's Cathedral, wandering through the Naschmarkt's vibrant stalls, or immersing yourself in the art collections of the Kunsthistorisches Museum, Vienna's offerings are as varied as the river's currents.

Every corner of Vienna reveals a new layer of history, art, and culture. From the romantic notes of a violin to the grandeur of imperial palaces, this city is an embodiment of the Danube's enchanting spirit. As your cruise adventure continues, let Vienna's melodies and masterpieces linger in your heart, a reminder of the timeless charm that awaits along the river's course.

Discovering Budapest's Delights

Budapest, the capital known as the "Pearl of the Danube," is a sensory feast that bridges the Buda and Pest sides of the river. The Hungarian Parliament Building stands as an architectural masterpiece, its neo-Gothic spires reaching towards the sky. As the sun sets, the city's bridges and landmarks illuminate, creating a romantic ambiance that sweeps you off your feet. Don't miss the thermal baths, where relaxation and rejuvenation await in the city's healing waters. As a beginner explorer, here's your handy guide to the must-see spots in Budapest as part of your unforgettable Danube cruise journey.

Buda Castle and Fisherman's Bastion:
Get your camera ready for Buda Castle, a majestic fortress that offers postcard-worthy views of the city. Nestled on Castle Hill, this historic gem is a great starting point. Nearby, the Fisherman's Bastion is like a fairy tale come to life. With its whimsical turrets and panoramic terraces, it's a photographer's dream.

Hungarian Parliament Building:
Prepare to be amazed by the grandeur of the Hungarian Parliament Building. Its impressive neo-Gothic architecture is a true masterpiece, especially when you see it illuminated at night. This iconic landmark reflects beautifully in the Danube, creating a scene you won't want to miss.

Chain Bridge and Danube Promenade:
Crossing the Chain Bridge is an experience you won't forget. Connecting Buda and Pest, it offers fantastic views of both sides of the city. For a leisurely stroll, head to the Danube Promenade. As the sun sets, the city's lights begin to twinkle, creating a magical atmosphere along the riverbank.

Széchenyi Thermal Bath:
Need a break from exploring? Treat yourself to relaxation at the Széchenyi Thermal Bath. These natural hot springs are not only soothing but also a unique cultural experience. Imagine unwinding in warm mineral-rich waters as you take in the beauty of Budapest.

Heroes' Square and City Park:
Heroes' Square is a monumental spot that showcases Hungary's history. With statues of national leaders and the Millennium Monument, it's a place of pride. Nearby City Park is perfect for a leisurely walk or even a boat ride on the lake. Don't forget to say hello to the resident ducks!

St. Stephen's Basilica and Great Market Hall:
St. Stephen's Basilica is a grand church with an impressive dome and stunning interiors. Climb to the top for a bird's-eye view of Budapest. To satisfy your taste buds, head to the Great Market Hall. This bustling marketplace is a feast for the senses, offering local treats and unique finds.

Ruin Bars and Nighttime Views:
As night falls, Budapest transforms into a vibrant playground. Ruin bars are a must-experience; these artistic and eccentric spaces redefine nightlife. For a magical evening, consider a dinner cruise. Sail along the Danube,

and witness the city's landmarks sparkle under the night sky.

Cultural Immersion in Bratislava and Belgrade: Where Traditions Thrive

As your cruise glides into Bratislava, the capital of Slovakia, you'll find a city that balances its rich history with a modern spirit. The Old Town's medieval architecture invites you to wander through narrow streets lined with colorful facades. Visit the imposing Bratislava Castle, a symbol of the city's resilience, and uncover the stories that have shaped Slovakia's identity.

Further downstream, the Serbian capital of Belgrade pulsates with energy. This vibrant metropolis is a blend of contrasts – where historic landmarks coexist with modern cafes and bustling markets. The Kalemegdan Fortress, overlooking the confluence of the Sava and Danube Rivers, offers a glimpse into the city's tumultuous past. As you navigate Belgrade's streets, you'll feel the heartbeat of a city that thrives on its cultural diversity.

Hidden Gems: Quaint Villages and Lesser-Known Stops - The Treasures Beyond the Headlines

Amidst the cities, the Danube reveals its hidden gems – charming villages and lesser-known stops that often carry stories as captivating as their larger counterparts. Dürnstein, a small Austrian village, captivates with its medieval allure. The ruins of Kuenringer Castle stand as silent witnesses to history, and the village's cobblestone streets lead you through a time capsule of tradition.

Passau, a picturesque town where three rivers meet, offers a blend of architectural marvels. The St. Stephen's Cathedral, with its impressive baroque dome, stands as a testament to the town's resilience in the face of floods. As you explore the town, you'll find echoes of its medieval past mingling with the vibrancy of its present.

Exploring Historic Castles and Landmarks - Tracing the Footsteps of Legends

The Danube's banks are adorned with historic castles and landmarks that transport you back in time. The Melk Abbey, an architectural masterpiece, crowns the Wachau Valley with its Baroque splendor. As you step into its hallowed halls, you'll sense the reverence of centuries past.

In Vienna, the Schönbrunn Palace invites you into the world of the Habsburgs. Wander through the lavishly furnished rooms, stroll in the meticulously landscaped gardens, and imagine the whispers of emperors and empresses that once graced these halls.

Further afield, the Bran Castle in Transylvania adds an air of mystery to your journey. Linked to the Dracula legend, the castle's turrets and towers beckon with tales of Count Dracula and the folklore that shrouds the region in a captivating aura.

An Odyssey of Stories and Experiences

As you traverse the Danube's path, each destination unfurls a new chapter of history, culture, and discovery. The cities, villages, and landmarks invite you to become a part of their narrative – to walk in the footsteps of emperors, to experience the music that echoes through Vienna's streets, to savor the flavors of Budapest's cuisine, and to embrace the traditions that thrive in the heart of Bratislava and Belgrade.

Your journey along the Danube is more than a cruise; it's an odyssey through time and place. It's an opportunity to uncover the layers of stories that have woven the fabric of Europe's history. So, as you set sail, open your heart and mind to the tales that await, and let the Danube's destinations paint a portrait of an unforgettable voyage.

Exploring the Charms of Prague

Congratulations on embarking on your Danube River cruise journey! As you set your course through the heart of Europe, another splendid destination awaits you: the captivating city of Prague. For beginners ready to discover its wonders, here's your essential guide to the must-see places in Prague as part of your unforgettable Danube cruise experience.

Prague Castle and St. Vitus Cathedral:
Prepare to be enchanted by Prague Castle, a true symbol of the city's history and grandeur. As you explore its courtyards and gardens, don't miss the awe-inspiring St. Vitus Cathedral. Its intricate Gothic architecture will leave you in awe, and the view from the tower is well worth the climb.

Charles Bridge and Old Town Square:
The iconic Charles Bridge is a true Prague landmark. Connecting the historic heart of the city, it's a picturesque spot to take a leisurely stroll. As you cross the bridge, you'll find yourself in Old Town Square. This charming area is

surrounded by stunning Gothic and Baroque buildings, including the Astronomical Clock. Be sure to watch it chime on the hour!

Josefov (Jewish Quarter) and Lennon Wall:
Take a step back in history in Josefov, the Jewish Quarter. Here, you'll find the hauntingly beautiful Old Jewish Cemetery and historic synagogues. For a more modern touch, visit the Lennon Wall. Covered in colorful graffiti and messages of peace, it's a testament to the enduring spirit of freedom and love.

Prague Astronomical Clock and Wenceslas Square:
The Prague Astronomical Clock, a mesmerizing medieval timepiece, is a must-see in Old Town Square. Join the crowd to watch the clock's hourly show. Nearby, Wenceslas Square is a bustling hub with shops, restaurants, and cultural events. This historic square has witnessed many of Prague's most important moments.

Petřín Hill and Prague Eiffel Tower:
For panoramic views of the city, head to Petřín Hill. You can hike up or take the funicular for a more leisurely ascent. At the top, you'll find an observation tower often called the "Prague Eiffel Tower." The views are breathtaking and perfect for those iconic vacation photos.

Czech Cuisine and Street Food:
Don't miss the chance to savor Czech cuisine. Try traditional dishes like goulash, schnitzel, and trdelník (a sweet pastry). And when you're on the go, explore street food options like klobása (sausage) or langos (fried dough). Pair your meal with a refreshing Czech beer for the full experience.

Exploring by Foot and Tram:
Prague's compact size makes it easy to explore on foot. Wander through the charming streets, and don't hesitate to venture into quieter neighborhoods. To cover more ground, hop on a tram - the city's public transportation system is efficient and convenient.

Nighttime Magic and Vltava River:
As the sun sets, Prague transforms into a magical wonderland. The beautifully lit buildings and bridges create an enchanting atmosphere. Take a stroll along the Vltava River, and consider a relaxing evening boat cruise. The illuminated landmarks reflected on the water will leave you with unforgettable memories.

Capture the Memories:
Finally, don't forget to capture the beauty of Prague. Every cobblestone street, every castle tower, and every friendly smile will tell a story. Your photos will serve as a delightful reminder of your journey through this captivating city.

In conclusion, Prague is a city that seamlessly weaves history and modernity, creating an atmosphere of wonder and discovery. As you disembark from your Danube cruise and step onto Prague's streets, let your curiosity guide you. With its rich heritage, stunning architecture, and vibrant culture, this city promises a treasure trove of experiences for beginners and seasoned travelers alike. Enjoy every moment of your Prague adventure, and may your Danube cruise be a journey filled with exploration and joy.

CHAPTER FOUR

Cultural Immersion in Bratislava and Belgrade

Belgrade, once a European capital overshadowed by its tumultuous history, has transformed into a thriving hub of growth and optimism. Its ancient roots, stretching back 6,000 years, are woven with tales of strife and sorrow. Nonetheless, the city has displayed remarkable resilience, constantly bouncing back and currently undergoing a vibrant cultural and creative renaissance.

Nestled at the crossroads of the Sava and Danube rivers on the Balkan Peninsula, Belgrade's allure doesn't rest in extravagant structures or sprawling parks. Instead, it pulsates with a complex identity, enriched by the legacies of generations and the enduring traditions of numerous conquerors. A fusion of Old World elegance and a touch of Eastern mystique, Belgrade embodies an eclectic fusion of cultural influences and architectural styles, creating a distinct and captivating atmosphere.

Unveiling the city's essence begins at Kalemegdan, the historical hill that was its original settlement. Now a captivating complex of historical edifices overlooking the Old Town (Stari Grad), this site offers insight into Belgrade's past. Within it, the Military Museum narrates the city's tumultuous history, spanning from its earliest encounters with Roman legions in the 1st century BC to the harrowing NATO bombardment lasting 78 consecutive days in 1999.

For those whose fascination leans more toward the contemporary, modern Belgrade offers an array of leisure and entertainment options. The famed nightclubs pulsate with techno beats, while the charm of bohemian Skadarlija Street is alive with restaurants and street performances. Visitors stepping into Belgrade will experience a warm embrace from the resilient and proud residents of this unyielding city, where history and the present merge seamlessly.

Bratislava, the capital of Slovakia, often falls under the radar despite being just an hour's journey from Vienna. This picturesque city boasts a captivating old-town ambiance, complete with charming cobbled streets and enchanting buildings that could be straight out of a fairy tale. It's home to two remarkable castles that should not be missed: Bratislava Castle, offering stunning vistas of the city, and Devin Castle, a photographer's dream with its Instagram-worthy ruins. With its compact size, Bratislava is a walker's paradise, allowing you to discover all the key attractions within a mere two days.

Bratislava's Charms:
Bratislava, the capital of Slovakia, is a gem that blends old-world charm with modern energy. As a beginner explorer, here's how you can make the most of your cultural journey:

Stroll Through the Old Town: Start by wandering through Bratislava's Old Town. With its cobblestone streets and colorful buildings, it's like stepping into a fairy tale. Take in the sights of medieval castles and Baroque palaces that line the charming squares.

Bratislava Castle: High above the city sits Bratislava Castle, a symbol of its history. Explore the castle grounds and soak in sweeping views of the Danube and the surrounding landscape.

Taste Local Flavors: Slovak cuisine is a delightful blend of hearty and comforting dishes. Try bryndzové halušky, a dish with potato dumplings and sheep cheese, for a true taste of Slovakia.

Belgrade's Vibrant Scene:
As your Danube cruise continues, Belgrade, the capital of Serbia, offers a rich tapestry of cultural experiences for beginners to enjoy:

Kalemegdan Fortress: Perched at the confluence of the Sava and Danube Rivers, Kalemegdan Fortress is both a historic monument and a beautiful park. Wander its paths, take in views of the rivers, and explore its intriguing history.

Bohemian Quarter: Skadarlija, the Bohemian Quarter of Belgrade, is a haven for art, music, and delicious food. Stroll along its cobbled streets, enjoy live music, and savor Serbian specialties.

Ada Ciganlija: If you're looking for a taste of local leisure, head to Ada Ciganlija, a river island turned peninsula. This recreational area offers beaches, bike paths, and a chance to join locals in their favorite pastimes.

Cultural Traditions: In both Bratislava and Belgrade, you'll find a strong connection to music, art, and history. Be open to engaging with locals and learning about their traditions.

From folk music performances to open-air markets, there's always something to discover.

Travel Tips for Cultural Immersion:

1. **Open-Mindedness:** Embrace the unfamiliar. Every sight, sound, and taste is a chance to learn and appreciate a new culture.

2. **Local Interactions:** Engage with locals through small conversations, even if it's just a smile and a nod. Locals often love sharing insights about their city.

3. **Try Local Fare:** Food is a gateway to culture. Don't shy away from trying traditional dishes – it's a delightful adventure for your taste buds.

4. **Attend Cultural Events:** Check if there are any local festivals, concerts, or exhibitions happening during your visit. These events offer authentic cultural experiences.

5. **Learn a Few Words:** A few basic phrases in the local language can go a long way in showing respect and making connections.

These enchanting villages and lesser-known stops invite you to explore their history, culture, and breathtaking landscapes. From hikes to hilltop castles to strolling through cobbled streets, each experience promises to deepen your connection with Europe's hidden treasures. As you navigate these destinations, may your voyage be a tapestry woven with moments of wonder and exploration. Bon voyage, adventurers!

These enchanting villages and lesser-known stops invite you to explore their history, culture, and breathtaking landscapes. From hikes to hilltop castles to strolling through cobbled streets, each experience promises to deepen your connection with Europe's hidden treasures. As you navigate these destinations, may your voyage be a tapestry woven with moments of wonder and exploration. Bon voyage, adventurers!

Lesser-Known Stops Along Your Danube River Cruise: Unveiling Hidden Treasures

Welcome, fellow adventurers, to the enchanting world of Danube River cruising! Beyond the awe-inspiring landscapes and bustling cities, lie hidden gems that beckon you to explore and discover the rich tapestry of Europe's culture and history. As you embark on this voyage of wonder, allow us to guide you through the alluring villages and lesser-known stops that add an extra layer of magic to your Danube River cruise experience. Let's set sail on a journey of exploration!

Dürnstein, Austria: Unveiling the Echoes of the Past

Why It's Cool: Perched high upon a hill, the ruins of Dürnstein Castle whisper tales of history, intrigue, and the captivity of none other than King Richard the Lionheart of England. During the Third Crusade, Duke Leopold V of Austria held the king captive in this very castle, creating an unforgettable chapter in history. As your Danube River cruise anchors at Dürnstein, prepare for a captivating guided hike up the hill to the rocky ridge. From the castle's vantage point, soak in commanding views of the vineyard-draped countryside—a sight to behold and a hike that's sure to reward your efforts.

Exploring the Port: The charming port itself rests serenely along the Danube's banks. With its quaint cobbled streets and a picturesque setting, it's a destination where time seems to stand still. Embark on delightful excursions that combine town exploration with tantalizing tastings of regional wines. Wander through the streets lined with inviting shops that offer local foods and unique souvenirs, creating memories to cherish.

Esztergom, Hungary: Discovering Majestic Grandeur
Why It's Cool: Nestled within Hungary, Esztergom reveals its historical significance with pride. Home to the grand Esztergom Basilica, one of the largest churches globally, the city boasts a domed structure that can be seen from miles away. This edifice of architectural splendor stands as a testament to the city's rich past and religious heritage. As you explore its museums and stroll along the Danube's tranquil banks, you'll uncover the layers of history that shaped this hidden gem.

Exploring the Port: The port of Esztergom invites you to delve into Hungary's storied past. Wander through its streets, engage with locals, and admire the architectural marvels that grace the city. As you explore, you'll find that beneath its peaceful surface, Esztergom holds a treasure trove of historical stories and cultural richness waiting to be explored.

Novi Sad, Serbia: A Cultural Kaleidoscope
Why It's Cool: Novi Sad, Serbia's cultural capital, brims with a vibrant energy and a blend of historic and modern charm. The Petrovaradin Fortress stands as a sentinel, offering panoramic views of the Danube and the city below. Novi Sad's streets come alive with bustling markets and festivals, creating an atmosphere that captivates the senses. Embrace the city's youthful spirit and immerse yourself in its artistic expressions.

Exploring the Port: Step into Novi Sad's lively streets and find a city that blends past and present seamlessly. From exploring the historical fortress to joining the locals in celebrations, you'll find that Novi Sad offers an immersive experience of Serbia's cultural diversity and creative pulse.

Visegrád, Hungary: A Glimpse into Medieval Majesty
Why It's Cool: Visegrád, set along the Danube's graceful curve, invites you to step back in time. The town's history is etched into its very fabric, with the Visegrád Castle standing as a sentinel to Hungary's medieval past. The hilltop setting of the castle provides a panoramic view that transports you to a world of kings and knights, set against nature's picturesque backdrop.

Exploring the Port: Visegrád's tranquil allure allows you to immerse yourself in its serene beauty. As you explore the ruins and absorb the ambiance, you'll find that the town holds a quiet charm that captures the essence of Hungary's history and natural splendor.

Melk, Austria: Where Baroque Meets Beauty

Why It's Cool: Melk, situated in the heart of Austria, is a testament to Baroque opulence. The grand Melk Abbey, a UNESCO World Heritage Site, beckons with its opulent interiors adorned with frescoes and sculptures. Stroll through its tranquil gardens and admire the grandeur of a bygone era brought to life.

Exploring the Port: Melk's serene ambiance provides a haven of tranquility. The abbey's grandeur and the town's allure invite you to explore at a leisurely pace, creating a sense of serenity amidst your journey.

Navigating the Hidden Treasures:
1. **Embrace the Stories:** Each stop holds a tale waiting to be discovered. Engage with guides and locals to uncover the narratives that shape these hidden treasures.

2. **Capture the Essence:** Photographs are more than just snapshots; they're windows into the soul of a place. Capture the unique beauty and character of each stop.

3. **Interact and Immerse:** Engage with the locals and embrace their traditions. From artisans to market vendors, their stories add a layer of authenticity to your experience.

4. **Savor Local Flavors:** Taste the regional cuisine and savor the flavors that define each destination. Culinary experiences connect you to the heart of a place.

5. **Pause and Reflect:** Amidst the exploration, take moments to pause and absorb the surroundings. The quiet moments often reveal the soul of a place.

CHAPTER FIVE

Unpacking and Cabin Tips for Your Danube River Cruise Adventure

Welcome aboard your Danube River cruise, a journey filled with breathtaking landscapes, cultural experiences, and unforgettable memories. As you settle into your cabin, we want to ensure that your voyage is as comfortable and enjoyable as possible. Here are some unpacking and cabin tips to help you make the most of your river cruise adventure.

1. Arriving and Getting Settled

After embarking on your Danube River cruise, you'll find your cabin ready and waiting for you. Take a moment to familiarize yourself with the layout – your home for the duration of this unforgettable journey. While cabins on river cruise ships are often cozier than those on ocean liners, they're designed with your comfort in mind.

2. Efficient Packing

Begin by unpacking essentials that you'll need during your journey. Keep frequently used items, like toiletries, in an easily accessible place. Utilize the closet space and drawers for clothing and accessories. Remember that river cruises are typically more relaxed in terms of dress codes, so pack comfortable and casual attire. A pair of sturdy walking shoes is a must for shore excursions.

3. Utilizing Cabin Storage

River cruise cabins are cleverly designed to maximize space. Make use of under-bed storage for suitcases and larger items. You'll find shelves and hooks for hanging clothes, as well as built-in storage for smaller items. Keeping your cabin tidy ensures a pleasant atmosphere and allows you to easily locate your belongings.

4. Staying Organized

As you unpack, consider using packing cubes or organizers to keep items categorized. This can help streamline your daily routine and save time when getting ready for shore excursions or onboard activities. Keeping things organized will also prevent the cabin from becoming cluttered.

5. Cabin Comfort and Personalization

Your cabin is your private oasis, and you can personalize it to suit your preferences. Feel free to bring along photos, books, or other small items that make you feel at home. Adjust the cabin temperature to your liking, and utilize the blackout curtains for a restful night's sleep.

6. Bathroom Essentials

River cruise ship cabins come equipped with en-suite bathrooms. You'll find towels, toiletries, and a hairdryer provided for your convenience. If you have specific toiletry preferences, you may want to bring your own products. It's also a good idea to pack a small first aid kit with essentials like pain relievers and motion sickness medication, just in case.

7. Electrical Outlets and Adapters

European river cruise ships typically have European-style electrical outlets. Be sure to bring the necessary adapters to charge your devices. Many modern river cruise ships also provide USB ports for charging, making it convenient to keep your gadgets powered.

8. Connecting with Wi-Fi

Most river cruise ships offer Wi-Fi connectivity in cabins and common areas. Keep in mind that river cruise Wi-Fi may not be as fast or stable as what you're used to on land. It's a good opportunity to disconnect and immerse yourself in the journey, but if you need to stay connected, plan accordingly.

9. Onboard Courtesy and Quiet Hours

While river cruise ships are designed to minimize noise between cabins, it's always a good practice to be considerate of your fellow travelers. Keep noise levels down during early morning and late evening hours, and avoid loud conversations or music in the corridors.

10. Safety First

As you settle into your cabin, take a moment to familiarize yourself with safety features, such as the location of life jackets and emergency exits. Your cruise staff will provide safety information during the ship's orientation, and it's essential to be prepared in case of any unforeseen situations.

11. Enjoying the Views

One of the joys of a river cruise is the ever-changing scenery. Take advantage of your cabin's window or balcony to admire the picturesque landscapes as they unfold. Whether it's the charming villages, lush vineyards, or historic castles, each view is a snapshot of the Danube's allure.

12. Unwind and Savor

Your cabin is not just a place to sleep; it's a space to unwind, reflect, and savor the moments of your river cruise adventure. Whether you're reading a book by the window, enjoying a cup of coffee on your balcony, or simply watching the world go by, your cabin is your personal retreat amidst the beauty of the Danube.

As you unpack and settle into your cabin, remember that your river cruise is a journey of discovery, comfort, and connection. Your cabin is more than just a room – it's a cozy haven that enhances your entire cruise experience. So, unpack, unwind, and embark on a voyage that promises to be a symphony of sights, sounds, and unforgettable memories along the Danube's enchanting waters.

Dining Delights: Onboard Culinary Experiences for Your Danube River Cruise Adventure

As you embark on your Danube River cruise, prepare to embark on a culinary journey that will awaken your taste buds and immerse you in the rich flavors of the regions you'll explore. From hearty breakfasts to gourmet dinners, every meal on board is an opportunity to savor the essence of the Danube's cultural diversity.

1. A Gastronomic Voyage Through Europe

Get ready to be delighted by the flavors of the Danube's banks. Onboard dining is a fusion of culinary traditions that reflect the regions you'll traverse. From the Hungarian spice of Budapest to the Austrian elegance of Vienna, each meal is an invitation to discover the culinary soul of Europe.

2. Breakfast: Energize Your Day

Start your mornings with a hearty breakfast that sets the tone for your adventures. Enjoy a buffet spread featuring freshly baked bread, pastries, cereals, yogurt, and a variety of fresh fruits. Made-to-order omelets and eggs, along with a selection of hot and cold beverages, ensure that you're fueled for the day ahead.

3. Lunch: A Tantalizing Exploration

Lunches on board are a chance to explore diverse flavors inspired by the regions you'll visit. Sample local ingredients and dishes that give you a taste of the culture and cuisine of each destination. From light salads to satisfying mains, lunch offers a well-rounded selection to satisfy every palate.

4. Dinner: A Gourmet Affair

Evenings bring the opportunity to indulge in gourmet creations that showcase the culinary expertise of the ship's chefs. Savor dishes inspired by local ingredients, expertly paired with wines that complement the flavors. The ship's elegant dining room provides a refined setting for a memorable dining experience.

5. Specialty Dining: Intimate Experiences

For a truly special evening, consider indulging in a specialty dining experience. These intimate settings offer curated menus that highlight the chef's creativity and expertise. Whether it's a chef's table dinner or an al fresco meal on the sun deck, specialty dining is a chance to elevate your culinary adventure.

6. Wine Tastings and Pairings: Toast to Tradition

Discover the art of wine appreciation through onboard wine tastings and pairings. Explore the nuances of local wines as expert sommeliers guide you through the tasting process. Learn about the winemaking traditions of the Danube region and savor the connection between the landscape and the wines it produces.

7. Dietary Considerations: Personalized Dining

Catering to dietary preferences and allergies is a priority on your Danube River cruise. Whether you're vegetarian, gluten-free, or have specific dietary restrictions, the onboard culinary team is ready to accommodate your needs. Notify the cruise staff in advance, and they'll ensure that your dining experience is both delicious and tailored to your requirements.

8. Communal Dining: Share the Experience

Communal dining tables create an atmosphere of camaraderie, allowing you to connect with fellow travelers over shared meals. Engage in conversations, exchange travel stories, and make new friends as you enjoy the pleasures of dining together. The dining room becomes a space for social connections that enhance your journey.

9. Culinary Memories: Beyond the Plate

The culinary experiences on your Danube River cruise are more than just meals; they're memories waiting to be savored. Each dish tells a story of the region, from the ingredients used to the techniques employed. The joy of breaking bread with new friends, the satisfaction of discovering a new favorite dish, and the shared laughter over a bottle of wine – these are the moments that make your dining experience unforgettable.

10. Embrace the Flavors of the Danube

From the first bite to the last sip, let the onboard culinary experiences be a centerpiece of your Danube River cruise adventure. Immerse yourself in the flavors of the regions, connect with the cultural heritage through your palate, and celebrate the culinary tapestry that spans the banks of the Danube. As you journey along this legendary river, the dining delights on board will be a symphony of tastes, textures, and memories that linger long after you disembark.

Entertainment and Activities During the Cruise: Enriching Your Danube River Experience

As you embark on your Danube River cruise, you're not only immersing yourself in captivating landscapes and cultural encounters – you're also stepping into a world of entertainment and activities that enrich every moment of your journey. From onboard enrichment lectures to lively evening entertainment, your cruise promises a diverse array of experiences that cater to every interest and preference. Let's explore the vibrant tapestry of entertainment and activities that await you along the Danube's winding waters.

1. Cultural Enrichment and Onboard Lectures

Your Danube River cruise is an opportunity to expand your horizons through enlightening onboard lectures and presentations. Engage with experts who share their insights into the history, art, and culture of the regions you're visiting. From the architecture of Vienna's palaces to the musical heritage of Budapest, these lectures provide a deeper understanding of the destinations that line the riverbanks.

2. Language and Cooking Workshops

Immerse yourself in the local culture through hands-on experiences such as language and cooking workshops. Learn a few key phrases in Hungarian or German, enhancing your interactions with locals during shore excursions. Alternatively, join a cooking demonstration led by the ship's chefs and discover the secrets behind iconic dishes from the Danube's countries.

3. Musical Performances and Onboard Entertainment

Evenings on the ship come alive with musical performances and onboard entertainment. Enjoy live music that ranges from traditional folk tunes to classical melodies. On special nights, experience the elegance of a Viennese waltz or the rhythm of Balkan folk dances. These performances transport you to the heart of the Danube's cultural heritage, making for enchanting and memorable evenings.

4. Sunset Views and Relaxation on the Sun Deck

The sun deck is a tranquil haven where you can unwind while admiring the ever-changing landscapes. Whether you're reading a book, soaking up the sun, or simply savoring the fresh river breeze, this space offers panoramic views that provide the perfect backdrop for relaxation. As the sun sets behind the horizon, the tranquil moments spent on the sun deck become cherished memories of your cruise.

5. Wine Tastings and Regional Workshops

Indulge in the flavors of the Danube by participating in wine tastings and regional workshops. Learn about the distinctive wines produced along the riverbanks and discover the nuances of local varietals. Whether you're a wine enthusiast or simply curious, these experiences offer a delightful way to connect with the region's terroir and traditions.

6. Fitness and Wellness Activities

Maintain your wellness routine with a range of onboard fitness activities. Join morning yoga sessions on the sun deck, engage in invigorating workouts, or take a leisurely stroll on the walking track while enjoying the scenic views. Keeping active during your cruise not only ensures you stay energized but also provides opportunities to appreciate the Danube's beauty from a different perspective.

7. Evening Social Gatherings and Games

After a day of exploration, evenings on board offer opportunities to socialize and unwind. Join fellow travelers for friendly card games, trivia competitions, or simply engage in lively conversations at the bar. These social gatherings foster connections that add depth to your cruise experience and create lasting friendships.

8. Captivating Film Screenings and Presentations

Engage with the region's history and culture through captivating film screenings and presentations. From documentaries that delve into the Danube's role in shaping Europe's past to presentations on contemporary issues, these sessions offer insights that complement your onshore experiences and expand your knowledge of the river's significance.

9. Stargazing and Astronomy Talks

As the ship glides along the Danube's tranquil waters, take advantage of the clear night skies for stargazing. Join astronomy talks and guided sessions that unveil the constellations and celestial wonders visible from the river. Whether you're an amateur astronomer or simply curious, the beauty of the night sky adds a touch of magic to your evenings on board.

10. Connecting with Nature and Wildlife Observation

The Danube River and its surroundings teem with wildlife and natural beauty. Engage in guided wildlife observation sessions, where experts share their knowledge of the river's diverse ecosystems. Keep an eye out for birds, aquatic creatures, and other inhabitants that call the Danube home, creating a deeper connection with the natural world around you.

11. Personal Reflection and Contemplation

The serene ambiance of the ship invites moments of personal reflection and contemplation. Find a quiet corner to enjoy a book, sketch the landscapes that inspire you, or simply watch the river flow by. These moments of solitude allow you to fully immerse yourself in the beauty of the Danube's landscapes and create a connection with the river's timeless rhythm.

12. Cultural Theme Nights and Costume Galas

Experience the vibrant cultures of the Danube's countries through themed nights and costume galas. Dress up in traditional attire or indulge in an evening of dancing that echoes the region's rich heritage. These themed events add a sense of festivity to your cruise, allowing you to celebrate the diverse cultures that shape the river's identity.

13. Crafting Lifelong Memories

As you partake in the diverse entertainment and activities on your Danube River cruise, you're not only creating memories but also crafting a rich narrative of your journey. Each lecture, musical performance, and moment of relaxation becomes a thread that weaves into the fabric of your cruise experience. Whether you're engaging with local traditions, discovering new passions, or simply finding moments of tranquility, the entertainment and activities on board contribute to a river cruise adventure that resonates long after you've returned home.

14. Embrace Every Experience

From sunrise to sunset, your Danube River cruise is a tapestry of experiences waiting to be embraced. Whether you're learning about the history of a castle, dancing to folk music, or gazing at the stars, each activity enriches your connection with the Danube and the regions it touches. So, as you navigate this river of stories, let the entertainment and activities on board be the melodies that enhance your journey.

Danube Festivals During the Cruise: Celebrating Culture and Traditions Along the River

Embarking on a Danube River cruise is not only a voyage through breathtaking landscapes and historic cities but also an opportunity to immerse yourself in the vibrant tapestry of local festivals and celebrations that line the riverbanks. From lively street fairs to centuries-old traditions, your cruise coinciding with these festivities offers a unique and enriching way to experience the culture and spirit of the Danube's diverse regions. Let's delve into the world of Danube festivals and discover how they can elevate your river cruise adventure.

1. Unveiling the Festival Calendar

The Danube River winds through a variety of countries, each with its own rich cultural heritage. Throughout the year, these nations come together to celebrate traditions, history, and local pride through a myriad of festivals. Whether it's a lively carnival in Germany or a wine festival in Austria's Wachau Valley, the festival calendar offers a window into the heart of each destination.

2. Carnival and Fasching Celebrations

If your Danube River cruise takes you through Germany, you might have the chance to experience Fasching, the German carnival season. This pre-Lenten celebration brings colorful parades, masquerade balls, and exuberant street parties to towns along the river. Don your own mask and join the revelry as you dance to traditional tunes and savor sweet treats that mark this joyous time of year.

3. Easter Markets and Traditions

Cruising the Danube during the Easter season unveils a world of charming Easter markets. These markets, found in cities like Vienna and Budapest, showcase handcrafted Easter decorations, intricate egg art, and delightful local pastries. Immerse yourself in the customs of each country as you explore these markets, enjoying the warm atmosphere and discovering unique souvenirs to take home.

4. Wine Festivals in the Wachau Valley

As your cruise navigates through Austria's Wachau Valley, you might find yourself in the midst of a local wine festival. These festivals celebrate the rich viticultural heritage of the region, offering an opportunity to sample exceptional wines, enjoy live music, and participate in traditional grape stomping ceremonies. Raise a glass with locals and fellow travelers alike, toasting to the joys of wine and the beauty of the Danube.

5. Summer Music Festivals

During the summer months, cities along the Danube host open-air music festivals that resonate with the sounds of classical, jazz, and folk music. Picture yourself attending a concert against the backdrop of Vienna's Schönbrunn

Palace or Budapest's Buda Castle. These performances bring the river's banks alive with melodies that reflect the region's musical legacy.

6. Medieval and Renaissance Fairs

Imagine stepping back in time as you visit medieval and Renaissance fairs along the Danube. With towns like Regensburg and Passau serving as hosts, these fairs transport you to eras of knights, jesters, and craftspeople. Explore historical reenactments, browse artisan stalls, and partake in traditional feasts that offer a glimpse into the past.

7. Harvest and Folk Festivals

Autumn brings a tapestry of colors to the Danube's landscapes, and it's also a time of harvest and folk celebrations. Explore local markets brimming with fresh produce, enjoy traditional music and dance performances, and witness the spirit of community that defines these festivals. The aroma of freshly baked bread and the sound of traditional instruments create an ambiance that's both festive and heartwarming.

8. Christmas Markets by the Danube

Cruising the Danube during the holiday season presents the opportunity to experience some of Europe's most enchanting Christmas markets. Explore the stalls adorned with twinkling lights, shop for handcrafted ornaments, and savor seasonal treats like mulled wine and gingerbread. The aroma of roasted chestnuts fills the air as you wander through the stalls, soaking up the magic of the festive season.

9. Folklore and Tradition

Throughout these festivals, you'll encounter the living heritage of the Danube's cultures. Participate in traditional dances, witness age-old rituals, and listen to stories that have been passed down through generations. These moments provide a deeper connection to the people and their history, allowing you to experience the authenticity of the region.

Danube River Cruises for Families: A Wholesome Adventure

Embarking on a Danube River cruise with your family is a journey that blends adventure, education, and relaxation into one unforgettable experience. As you set sail along the historic waterway, you'll find a wealth of opportunities for bonding, exploration, and creating lasting memories together. This guide is designed to help families navigate the exciting world of Danube River cruises, from choosing the right cruise and destination to considering prices and planning for a hassle-free vacation.

1. Finding the Perfect Cruise for Your Family

When selecting a Danube River cruise for your family, it's essential to consider the cruise line, ship amenities, and the destinations along the route. Many cruise lines offer family-friendly options that cater to different age groups with dedicated kids' clubs, entertainment, and educational activities. Research and compare cruise lines to ensure you choose one that aligns with your family's preferences and needs.

2. Onboard Amenities for All Ages

Modern Danube River cruise ships are designed to provide comfort and enjoyment for travelers of all ages. From well-appointed cabins and dining options to onboard entertainment and relaxation areas, the ship becomes a floating haven for families. Look for amenities like swimming pools, observation decks, and lounges that offer spaces for families to unwind and spend quality time together.

3. Family-Focused Shore Excursions

One of the highlights of a Danube River cruise is the opportunity to explore historic towns, cultural landmarks, and natural wonders along the way. Family-focused shore excursions provide enriching experiences for children and adults alike. Guided tours, interactive workshops, and visits to castles and museums offer a chance to learn about the regions you're visiting while keeping everyone engaged and entertained.

4. Destination Highlights

The Danube River flows through a diverse range of destinations, each with its own unique charm and history. From the imperial splendor of Vienna to the fairy-tale landscapes of the Wachau Valley and the vibrant streets of Budapest, your family will be captivated by the richness of the regions you'll explore. Consider your family's interests – whether it's history, culture, outdoor activities, or culinary experiences – when choosing your itinerary.

5. Considering Costs and Budget

Pricing for Danube River cruises varies based on factors such as cruise length, cabin type, cruise line, and inclusions. While family cruises may have higher costs due to added amenities and family-friendly programming, they often provide excellent value for the experiences offered. It's essential to factor in all-inclusive features, such as meals, entertainment, and guided tours, to accurately assess the overall cost.

6. Sample Prices of Popular Cruises

- A 7-night Danube River cruise from Budapest to Passau can start at around $2,000 per person for a standard cabin, with children often receiving discounted rates or sailing for free, depending on the cruise line and time of booking.

- Family-focused cruises with dedicated kids' activities and entertainment may have slightly higher prices, averaging around $2,500 to $3,500 per person for a week-long voyage.

- Suites and upgraded cabin options provide added space and comfort and typically come at a premium, ranging from $3,500 to $6,000 per person or more.

7. Budgeting Tips

To make the most of your Danube River cruise budget, consider the following:

- **Early Booking:** Many cruise lines offer early booking discounts, so plan ahead to secure the best rates.

- **Off-Peak Travel:** Shoulder seasons (spring and fall) often provide more affordable rates and fewer crowds.

- **Inclusions:** All-inclusive packages can help you stick to your budget by covering meals, excursions, and entertainment.

- **Kids' Discounts:** Look for cruise lines that offer discounted or free rates for children sharing a cabin with adults.

8. Planning and Preparation

Before embarking on your family Danube River cruise, make sure to:

- **Check Travel Documentation:** Ensure that everyone in your family has the required passports and visas for the destinations you'll be visiting.

- **Health and Safety:** Familiarize yourself with any health and safety guidelines related to your travel dates and destinations.

- **Pack Wisely:** Pack essentials for all family members, including comfortable walking shoes, weather-appropriate clothing, and any necessary medications.

- **Travel Insurance:** Consider purchasing travel insurance to protect your investment in case of unforeseen circumstances.

9. Capturing Cherished Moments

A family Danube River cruise is an opportunity to create cherished memories that will be treasured for years to come. From sharing meals in the ship's dining room to exploring charming towns hand in hand, the journey offers a chance to bond and share unique experiences with your loved ones. Don't forget to capture these moments through photos and journaling to relive the magic long after the cruise ends.

10. A Voyage of Discovery

A Danube River cruise for families is a journey that unfolds with discovery and delight. From the captivating landscapes to the immersive cultural experiences, your family will embark on an adventure that brings history, culture, and togetherness to the forefront. As you watch the shores of the Danube pass by, you'll witness not only the stunning vistas but also the joy on your family's faces – a testament to the magic of exploring the world together along this storied waterway.

Staying Connected on Your Danube River Cruise: Navigating the World of Internet Access

In today's interconnected world, staying connected during your Danube River cruise is a priority for many travelers. While embarking on this voyage of exploration, relaxation, and cultural immersion, maintaining access to the internet can enhance your experience by keeping you in touch with loved ones and allowing you to share your journey. This guide is designed to help you navigate the realm of internet access on Danube River cruises, from understanding connectivity options to considering costs and planning for a seamless online experience.

1. Understanding Onboard Internet Options

Danube River cruise ships are equipped with onboard internet services to cater to the connectivity needs of passengers. However, it's important to note that the level of internet access and speed may vary based on the cruise line, ship, and itinerary. Some ships offer complimentary Wi-Fi in common areas, while others provide more comprehensive packages that allow access from cabins as well.

2. Connecting to the World

Staying connected on your Danube River cruise offers several advantages:

- **Communication:** Keeping in touch with family and friends is essential, especially when you're away from home for an extended period.

- **Sharing Experiences:** Sharing photos, updates, and experiences on social media can help you capture and relive the magic of your journey.

- **Navigation and Research:** Accessing maps, travel apps, and local information online can enhance your onshore experiences.

3. Wi-Fi Access and Connectivity

Most Danube River cruise ships offer Wi-Fi access in designated areas such as lounges, common spaces, and sometimes in cabins. The connection speed may vary, and it's important to manage your expectations, as the internet on board may not be as fast or consistent as what you're accustomed to on land.

4. Considerations for Internet Use

When planning to stay connected during your Danube River cruise, consider the following:

- **Usage Patterns:** Determine how frequently and extensively you'll need internet access. This will help you choose the most suitable package.

- **Data Usage:** Streaming videos, downloading large files, and excessive use of social media can quickly deplete data allowances.

- **Privacy and Security:** Using public Wi-Fi networks comes with some security risks. Avoid accessing sensitive information or conducting financial transactions on public networks.

- **Roaming Charges:** If your cruise takes you to different countries, be mindful of potential roaming charges when using your mobile data plan.

5. Internet Packages and Costs

Internet packages on Danube River cruises are typically available for purchase, and the cost may vary depending on the cruise line and ship. Cruise lines may offer a variety of packages to suit different needs, ranging from basic social media access to more comprehensive plans that allow for streaming and larger data usage.

6. Sample Internet Package Prices

- Basic Social Media Package: Prices for basic packages that provide access to social media platforms and limited web browsing can start at around $10 per day.

- Standard Package: A more comprehensive package that includes web browsing and email access may range from $20 to $30 per day.

- Premium Package: For those who require higher speeds and more extensive data usage, premium packages can range from $30 to $50 per day.

7. Planning and Booking

When considering an internet package for your Danube River cruise:

- **Pre-Book:** Some cruise lines offer discounts for pre-booking internet packages before your cruise begins.

- **Select the Right Package:** Choose a package that aligns with your connectivity needs to avoid unnecessary costs.

- **Check for Promotions:** Keep an eye out for special promotions or offers that may provide added value for internet access.

8. Disconnecting Deliberately

While staying connected has its benefits, remember to strike a balance between staying online and fully immersing yourself in the cruise experience. The Danube River offers a chance to disconnect from the digital world and connect with the stunning landscapes, historic towns, and enriching cultural experiences that surround you.

9. Embrace the Journey

Staying connected on your Danube River cruise is a choice that depends on your personal preferences and priorities. Whether you opt for a comprehensive internet package or choose to limit your online activities, the most important thing is to embrace the journey and create lasting memories along the storied course of the Danube River.

10. Enriching Moments, In-Person and Online

The Danube River cruise experience is about more than just internet access – it's about immersing yourself in the beauty of the regions you'll explore, connecting with fellow travelers, and embracing the sense of wonder that comes with discovery. Balancing online interactions with in-person experiences allows you to capture the essence of the journey while keeping loved ones updated and engaged.

11. A Journey Beyond the Pixels

As you sail along the Danube's meandering waters, consider that the real voyage is the one that takes you beyond the pixels of a screen. Engage with the local culture, absorb the history, and savor the flavors. Use the internet as a tool to enhance your journey, but don't let it overshadow the magic of being present in the moment, surrounded by the beauty and wonder of the Danube River and its captivating destinations.

Packing Smart for Your Danube River Cruise: Essentials for a Memorable Voyage

Preparing for a Danube River cruise requires careful consideration of what to pack to ensure you have everything you need for a comfortable and enjoyable journey. From versatile clothing options to travel essentials, this guide will help you navigate the art of packing for your Danube adventure, ensuring that you're well-prepared for the diverse experiences that await you along the iconic European waterway.

1. Dressing for Comfort and Style

When packing for your Danube River cruise, keep in mind that you'll experience a mix of casual sightseeing, onboard dining, and special excursions. Here's a comprehensive packing list to guide you:

- **Casual Attire:** Comfortable clothing like jeans, shorts, t-shirts, and casual dresses are perfect for exploring charming towns and cities along the Danube.

- **Semi-Formal Wear:** Pack a few dressier options, such as a collared shirt, blouse, or a nice dress for evening dinners or onboard events.

- **Outerwear:** Bring a light jacket or sweater for cooler evenings and layers that you can easily add or remove depending on the weather.

- **Comfortable Shoes:** A pair of comfortable walking shoes is essential for exploring cobblestone streets and participating in shore excursions.

- **Formal Attire (Optional):** Some cruise lines may host formal nights. If you choose to participate, bring a suit or cocktail dress.

2. Essentials for Every Day

Certain items are crucial for ensuring your comfort and convenience during your Danube River cruise:

- **Travel Documents:** Passports, visas, cruise tickets, and any necessary identification are a must.

- **Medications:** Bring your prescribed medications, along with a small first aid kit for minor ailments.

- **Electronics:** Don't forget your camera, smartphone, charger, and power adapter if needed.

- **Reusable Water Bottle:** Stay hydrated during your excursions by carrying a reusable water bottle.

- **Sunglasses and Sunscreen:** Protect yourself from the sun's rays during outdoor activities.

- **Rain Gear:** Pack a compact umbrella or a waterproof jacket for unexpected rain.

3. Onboard Comfort and Relaxation

While you'll be exploring the destinations along the Danube, you'll also spend time onboard your cruise ship. Here are a few items to make your onboard experience more enjoyable:

- **Swimsuit:** If your cruise ship has a pool or spa area, a swimsuit will come in handy.

- **Comfortable Loungewear:** Pack comfortable clothing for lounging in your cabin or onboard common areas.

- **Entertainment:** Bring books, e-readers, puzzles, or other forms of entertainment for leisurely moments.

- **Slippers or Comfortable Shoes:** Having comfortable footwear for your cabin and onboard relaxation areas is a small but thoughtful addition.

4. Practical Accessories and Essentials

Several accessories and essentials can enhance your overall experience during your Danube River cruise:

- **Daypack or Tote Bag:** A lightweight bag for carrying essentials during shore excursions is invaluable.

- **Travel Wallet:** Keep your travel documents, cards, and cash organized and easily accessible.

- **Toiletries:** Travel-sized toiletries, including shampoo, conditioner, toothpaste, and sunscreen, ensure you have all your personal care needs covered.

- **Hand Sanitizer and Wet Wipes:** Useful for staying clean and refreshed during your travels.

- **Ziplock Bags:** These can be handy for storing wet items or protecting important documents.

5. Seasonal Considerations

The weather along the Danube can vary depending on the time of year you're cruising. Consider these seasonal tips:

- **Spring and Fall:** Pack layers to adapt to changing temperatures, and don't forget a rain jacket or umbrella.

- **Summer:** Lightweight clothing, sunscreen, a hat, and sunglasses are essential to beat the summer heat.

- **Winter:** If you're cruising during the colder months, bring warm clothing, a heavy coat, gloves, and a scarf.

6. Packing Tips and Tricks

- **Rolling vs. Folding:** Rolling your clothes can help save space and reduce wrinkles.

- **Use Packing Cubes:** These help keep your belongings organized and compact.

- **Check Luggage Allowances:** Be aware of your cruise line's luggage restrictions to avoid any surprises.

- **Leave Room for Souvenirs:** If you plan to shop, leave some extra space in your luggage for souvenirs and gifts.

7. Cruising in Style

As you pack for your Danube River cruise, remember that the key to a successful trip is a balance between preparedness and simplicity. Consider the destinations you'll visit, the activities you'll engage in, and the comfort you'll need both onboard and ashore. By packing wisely, you'll set the stage for an unforgettable journey along the storied waters of the Danube, where history, culture, and breathtaking landscapes await your exploration.

CHAPTER SIX
Navigation on the Danube River

Embarking on a Danube River cruise is a journey of exploration and discovery, offering the chance to immerse yourself in the beauty and history of Europe's iconic waterway. Navigating the Danube is an exciting experience, especially for beginners, as the river is renowned for its relatively calm and straightforward waters. However, understanding a few key aspects of navigation and safety precautions is essential to ensure a smooth and enjoyable journey.

1. River Characteristics and Considerations

The Danube River, while generally gentle, presents certain characteristics that can impact navigation:

- **Tidal Fluctuations:** The Danube is a tidal river, which means that its water level can fluctuate. These changes can influence the depth of the river and the speed of the current. Cruise ships are equipped to handle these variations, but it's important for passengers to be aware of potential shifts.

- **Locks and Dams:** The Danube River is dotted with locks and dams that regulate water levels and facilitate navigation. When a ship approaches a lock, it needs to wait for the lock to open before continuing its journey. These stops can add an interesting twist to your cruise, as you observe the inner workings of these engineering marvels.

- **Commercial Traffic:** The Danube is a bustling waterway with a significant amount of commercial traffic, including cargo ships and barges. While cruise ships have the right of way, it's essential to be attentive and cautious, especially when navigating through narrower passages or when sharing water space with larger vessels.

2. Safety Precautions for a Smooth Voyage

Ensuring your safety and that of your fellow passengers is paramount during your Danube River cruise. Here are some safety precautions to keep in mind:

- **Stay Informed:** Familiarize yourself with the daily cruise schedule, including port stops, shore excursions, and onboard activities. Pay attention to any announcements made by the ship's crew regarding navigation updates.

- **Obey Crew Instructions:** The ship's captain and crew are experienced navigators who prioritize the safety and well-being of passengers. Follow their instructions and guidelines for your safety and comfort.

- **Stay Alert:** While the Danube River is generally calm, the water's behavior can change due to tidal influences, wind, and other factors. Pay attention to your surroundings and the ship's movements, especially when transitioning through locks or encountering varying currents.

- **Wear Appropriate Footwear:** Comfortable and non-slip footwear is essential for moving around the ship's decks. This is particularly important during navigation and when participating in shore excursions.

- **Life Jacket Awareness:** Familiarize yourself with the location of life jackets in your cabin and public areas. While incidents are rare, it's always wise to know how to access safety equipment in case of emergency.

- **Stay Hydrated:** During warm weather or while exploring onshore, stay hydrated to maintain your well-being and comfort.

Cultural Treasures Along the Danube: Exploring Museums and Art Galleries

A Danube River cruise not only allows you to savor the beauty of picturesque landscapes and historic towns but also presents an opportunity to immerse yourself in the rich cultural tapestry of the regions you'll visit. Museums and art galleries along the Danube offer a glimpse into centuries of history, artistry, and cultural heritage.

1. The Belvedere Palace, Vienna (Austria)

The Belvedere Palace is a masterpiece of Baroque architecture that houses an impressive collection of Austrian art. It is home to the world's largest collection of works by Gustav Klimt, including the iconic painting "The Kiss." Wander through the opulent halls and manicured gardens, and witness the fusion of art and architecture in this cultural treasure.

2. Hungarian National Museum, Budapest (Hungary)

Immerse yourself in Hungary's history and heritage at the Hungarian National Museum. The museum showcases an extensive collection of artifacts, artworks, and historical objects that span the country's history from ancient times to the present. Explore the halls dedicated to archaeology, medieval art, and the revolution of 1956.

3. The Buda Castle, Budapest (Hungary)

Perched atop a hill overlooking the Danube, the Buda Castle is not only an architectural marvel but also a cultural hub. Inside its walls, you'll find the Hungarian National Gallery, which houses an impressive collection of Hungarian art spanning from the Middle Ages to the present day. The gallery offers a comprehensive overview of the country's artistic evolution.

4. Slovak National Gallery, Bratislava (Slovakia)

The Slovak National Gallery is a showcase of Slovak visual art, spanning centuries of creativity and expression. From medieval art to contemporary works, the gallery provides insights into the nation's cultural journey. Explore its diverse exhibitions, which include painting, sculpture, decorative arts, and more.

5. Kunsthistorisches Museum, Vienna (Austria)

The Kunsthistorisches Museum in Vienna is a testament to the grandeur of the Habsburg dynasty. Its magnificent interiors house an extensive collection of art and artifacts from around the world. From Egyptian and Greek antiquities to masterpieces by the likes of Rembrandt,

Vermeer, and Raphael, this museum is a treasure trove of artistic wonders.

6. Serbian Academy of Sciences and Arts, Belgrade (Serbia)

Immerse yourself in Serbian culture at the Serbian Academy of Sciences and Arts. This institution promotes and preserves the country's cultural heritage through its collections of art, manuscripts, and rare books. It's a window into the literary, scientific, and artistic contributions of Serbia.

7. Vienna's Albertina Museum and Art Gallery (Austria)

The Albertina is a renowned institution housing a remarkable collection of graphic arts, spanning from the Renaissance to the present day. Discover masterpieces by artists like Leonardo da Vinci, Albrecht Dürer, and Michelangelo, as well as modern works by Picasso, Klimt, and Schiele.

Tips for Exploring Museums and Galleries
Plan Ahead: Research the opening hours, admission fees, and highlights of the museums and galleries you plan to visit.

- Guided Tours: Many museums offer guided tours that provide insights into the exhibits and historical context. Consider joining a tour to enhance your understanding.
- Audio Guides: Audio guides are a valuable tool for self-guided exploration, providing additional information about the artworks and artifacts.

- Cultural Etiquette: Respect the rules and regulations of each museum or gallery, including photography policies and dress codes.
- Check for Special Exhibitions: Some museums host temporary exhibitions that may align with your interests. Check their websites for current offerings.
- Local Insights: Don't hesitate to engage with locals and fellow travelers for recommendations on must-visit cultural institutions.

Navigating Local Customs and Etiquette: Embracing Cultural Sensibilities Along the Danube

Embarking on a Danube River cruise is a journey that not only allows you to explore picturesque landscapes and historic sites but also provides an opportunity to engage with the rich tapestry of cultures that line the river's shores. As you visit diverse countries and immerse yourself in the local way of life, understanding and respecting local customs and etiquette is essential to ensure meaningful interactions and a seamless travel experience. In this guide, we'll navigate the nuances of embracing local customs and etiquette along the Danube, enhancing your journey with authentic connections and cultural sensitivity.

Cultural Diversity Along the Danube

The Danube River flows through a multitude of countries, each with its own distinct cultural identity and customs. From the elegant sophistication of Vienna to the vibrant energy of Budapest, and from the historic charm of Bratislava to the artistic spirit of Belgrade, the regions along the Danube offer a rich mosaic of cultural experiences. Embracing local customs and etiquette not only shows respect for the host culture but also enriches your travel experience by fostering genuine connections with locals.

1. Greetings and Introductions

Austria: A handshake is the standard form of greeting. Maintain eye contact and use formal titles unless invited to use first names.

Hungary: A handshake is common, and close friends may exchange a kiss on each cheek. Address people using their titles and last names.

Slovakia: A firm handshake is the norm, and it's polite to wait for a woman to extend her hand first. Use titles and last names unless invited to do otherwise.

Serbia: A warm handshake is customary, and greetings may include inquiries about well-being. Address people using their titles and last names, and expect personal questions as a sign of interest.

2. Dining Etiquette

Austria: Table manners are formal, and it's customary to wait for the host to start eating. Rest your wrists on the edge of the table, keeping your hands visible.

Hungary: Wait for the host to initiate the meal, and keep your hands above the table. Finish all the food on your plate to show appreciation for the meal.

Slovakia: Wait for the host's cue before beginning the meal. Keep your hands on the table, but avoid resting your elbows on it.

Serbia: Wait for the host to start the meal and keep your hands on the table. It's polite to finish everything on your plate, signaling your enjoyment.

3. Dressing Appropriately

Austria: Dress neatly and conservatively, especially when visiting religious sites or formal venues.

Hungary: Dress well when in public places. Casual attire is acceptable in most situations, but consider dressing slightly more formally for dinners and cultural events.

Slovakia: Dress modestly and avoid revealing clothing, especially when visiting religious sites or formal occasions.

Serbia: Dressing well is important, and it's customary to dress more formally for evening outings or cultural events.

4. Gift Giving

Austria: Flowers, chocolates, or a bottle of wine are suitable gifts when visiting someone's home. Always give odd numbers of flowers, as even numbers are associated with funerals.

Hungary: Bring a small gift for the host when invited to someone's home. Flowers or a box of chocolates are thoughtful choices.

Slovakia: When invited to someone's home, bring a gift such as flowers, chocolates, or wine. It's polite to give odd numbers of flowers.

Serbia: Small gifts such as chocolates or flowers are appreciated when visiting someone's home. Avoid giving lilies, as they are associated with funerals.

5. Cultural Sensitivity

Religious Sites: When visiting churches or religious sites, dress modestly and follow any rules or guidelines for visitors. Avoid loud conversations and respect the sanctity of the space.

Language: Learning a few basic phrases in the local language, such as greetings and thank you, can go a long way in showing respect and building rapport.

Tipping: Familiarize yourself with local tipping customs, as they may vary from country to country. In most cases, a 10-15% tip is appreciated in restaurants.

Be Open and Respectful

As you cruise along the Danube and explore the captivating destinations it touches, remember that cultural sensitivity is a bridge to meaningful connections. By embracing local customs and etiquette, you'll not only show respect for the cultures you encounter but also create memorable interactions and a deeper understanding of the people who call the Danube's banks home. As you embark on this journey of cultural exploration, your willingness to learn, adapt, and engage will enhance your experience and enrich your memories along the storied river.

Bridging Cultures Through Language: Engaging with Locals Along the Danube
Embarking on a Danube River cruise is not just a journey through stunning landscapes and historic sites – it's also an opportunity to connect with the people who call the river's banks home. While English is widely spoken in many of the regions you'll visit, making an effort to speak a few local phrases can go a long way in fostering genuine connections and showing respect for the cultures you encounter. In this guide, we'll navigate the world of language and offer tips on how to engage with locals along the Danube, enhancing your travel experience and leaving a positive impact on the communities you visit.

1. Embrace Basic Phrases

Learning a few basic phrases in the local language is a wonderful way to break the ice and show your genuine interest in connecting with locals. Here are some essential phrases to consider:

- **Greetings:** Mastering greetings like "hello," "good morning," and "good evening" can instantly make interactions more personal. In German-speaking areas (Austria and parts of Germany), "Guten Tag" (good day) and "Danke" (thank you) are valuable phrases.

- **Asking for Help:** Simple phrases like "Excuse me," "Can you help me?", and "Where is the (insert place)?" can be incredibly useful for navigation and information-seeking.

- **Courtesy Phrases:** Expressions like "please," "thank you," and "you're welcome" transcend language barriers and show respect and gratitude.

2. Cultural Sensitivity

When using local phrases, be aware of cultural context and appropriateness. If unsure, observe how locals greet each other and follow suit. It's essential to use appropriate language in formal situations, such as addressing people with titles and last names.

3. Language Learning Apps and Tools

Before your cruise, consider using language learning apps or guides to familiarize yourself with key phrases. Apps like

Duolingo, Babbel, or Memrise offer interactive lessons that can boost your confidence in speaking the local language.

4. Engaging with Locals

When engaging with locals, your effort to communicate in their language often elicits smiles and appreciation. Here's how to make the most of these interactions:

- **Greet and Smile:** Begin conversations with a friendly greeting and a genuine smile. This sets a positive tone and shows your eagerness to connect.

- **Ask Permission:** Before launching into the local language, ask if the person speaks English. If not, your attempt to speak their language will be even more appreciated.

- **Speak Slowly:** If you're not fluent in the language, speak slowly and clearly. This helps locals understand you better, and they may reciprocate by speaking slowly as well.

- **Use Nonverbal Communication:** Gestures, expressions, and body language are powerful tools for communication. Combine them with your spoken words for better understanding.

5. Experiencing Authenticity

Engaging with locals in their language opens doors to authentic experiences that you might otherwise miss. Here's how language can enrich your journey:

- **Navigating Markets:** Bargaining at local markets becomes more enjoyable when you can communicate with vendors in their language.

- **Ordering Food:** Trying local cuisine is a highlight of any journey. Ordering in the local language not only enhances your dining experience but also shows respect for the culinary heritage.

- **Asking for Recommendations:** Locals often have the best insights on hidden gems and local favorites. Conversing in their language can lead to valuable recommendations.

- **Cultural Exchange:** Engaging with locals allows you to learn about their way of life, traditions, and perspectives. These insights provide a deeper connection to the places you visit.

6. Enjoy the Journey

While making an effort to speak the local language is appreciated, remember that the goal is to enhance your travel experience and connect with locals. Even if you encounter language barriers, don't hesitate to use gestures, smiles, and friendly demeanor to bridge gaps and create meaningful interactions.

A World of Connections Awaits

The Danube River cruise is not just a voyage through landscapes but a journey through cultures. Engaging with locals in their language is a bridge to those cultures, allowing you to immerse yourself in the heart of each destination. By learning a few key phrases, you're opening doors to deeper connections, authentic experiences, and memories that go beyond the surface. As you travel along the Danube's storied waters, let language be your key to unlocking the beauty of human connection and understanding.

Understanding the Danube's Rich Cultural Tapestry

The Danube River is a cultural melting pot, with a rich history and diverse cultures. The river flows through 10 countries, each with its own unique culture and history. This has led to a diverse and vibrant cultural tapestry along the Danube.

Some of the most notable cultural influences along the Danube River include:

- The Roman Empire, which built many cities and towns along the river, and whose language and culture spread throughout the region.

- The Byzantine Empire, which brought its own unique culture to the region, which influenced the development of local cultures.

- The Ottoman Empire, which ruled over much of the Danube region for over 500 years, and whose culture and religion had a major impact on local cultures.

- The cultures of Central Europe, which blended with local cultures.

- The cultures of Eastern Europe, which have had a major impact on the region.

Today, the Danube River region is home to a diverse and vibrant cultural tapestry. This diversity is reflected in the architecture, food, music, and festivals of the region.

A Danube River cruise is a great way to experience this rich cultural heritage. Visitors can learn about the diverse cultures that have shaped the region by visiting historical sites, attending cultural events, and tasting traditional foods.

Here are some specific examples of the cultural diversity along the Danube River:

- In Vienna, Austria, visitors can visit the Hofburg Palace, the former home of the Habsburg emperors, and enjoy a performance at the Vienna Opera House.

- In Budapest, Hungary, visitors can visit the Buda Castle, which offers stunning views of the city, and take a walk along the Danube Promenade.

- In Bratislava, Slovakia, visitors can visit the Bratislava Castle, which is perched on a hill overlooking the city, and take a walk through the Old Town.

- In Belgrade, Serbia, visitors can visit the Kalemegdan Fortress, which is one of the oldest fortifications in the city, and take a walk along the Danube River.

These are just a few examples of the many cultural experiences that can be found along the Danube River. A Danube River cruise is a great way to experience this rich cultural heritage and to learn about the diverse cultures that have shaped the region.

Savoring the Flavors of the Danube: Culinary Delights on Your River Cruise

Embarking on a Danube River cruise is not just a journey through history and culture – it's also a culinary exploration that tantalizes your taste buds with a rich tapestry of flavors. As you traverse the enchanting cities and towns along the river, you'll have the opportunity to savor a diverse array of dishes that reflect the gastronomic heritage of the region. In this guide, we'll navigate the world of Danube River cuisine, highlighting the culinary delights that await you and offering tips on how to make the most of your culinary journey.

1. A Culinary Journey Along the Danube

The Danube River cruise promises a gastronomic adventure that spans across countries, cultures, and culinary traditions. Each destination you visit will introduce you to unique flavors, ingredients, and dining experiences that capture the essence of the region.

2. Regional Specialties

From hearty stews to delicate pastries, the Danube River region is brimming with iconic dishes that reflect the history and culture of the area. Here are some culinary highlights to savor:

- **Wiener Schnitzel (Austria):** A tender veal or pork cutlet, breaded and fried to golden perfection. It's a classic Austrian dish that pairs well with potato salad or lingonberry sauce.

- **Goulash (Hungary):** A hearty stew made with tender beef, paprika, onions, and other spices. Enjoy it with a side of Hungarian dumplings or crusty bread.

- **Lángos (Hungary):** A popular street food, lángos is deep-fried dough served with various toppings, such as sour cream, cheese, and garlic.

- **Slovak Bryndzové Halušky (Slovakia):** These potato dumplings are topped with bryndza cheese and bacon, creating a comforting and flavorful dish.

- **Sarma (Serbia):** Cabbage leaves stuffed with a mixture of ground meat, rice, and spices, simmered in a tomato-based sauce.

3. Danube Wines and Beverages

The Danube River region is also known for its wines and beverages that complement its culinary offerings:

- **Wachau Valley Wines (Austria):** The Wachau Valley is renowned for its white wines, particularly Grüner Veltliner and Riesling. Take the opportunity to sample local wines during your journey.

- **Tokaji Wine (Hungary):** Indulge in the legendary sweet dessert wine, Tokaji, which boasts a rich history and unique production process.

- **Slivovitz (Serbia):** A strong fruit brandy made from plums, Slivovitz is a traditional Serbian spirit often enjoyed as an aperitif or after a meal.

4. Dining Experiences

As you journey along the Danube, you'll encounter a variety of dining experiences that range from traditional to contemporary:

- **Local Eateries:** Venture beyond the main tourist areas to discover local eateries where you can savor authentic dishes favored by locals.

- **Market Visits:** Explore bustling local markets to sample fresh produce, cheeses, meats, and pastries that showcase the region's culinary diversity.

- **Onboard Dining:** Your river cruise ship will likely offer a range of dining options, including formal dinners, buffets, and themed meals that highlight regional cuisine.

5. Dining Etiquette

Understanding local dining etiquette adds an extra layer of enjoyment to your culinary experiences:

- **Austrian Dining Etiquette:** Maintain a formal demeanor during meals and use utensils correctly. Wait for the host to start eating before you begin.

- **Hungarian Dining Etiquette:** It's polite to make a toast before starting the meal. Don't begin eating until the host initiates.

- **Slovak Dining Etiquette:** Wait for the host to start eating and keep your hands on the table, but avoid resting your elbows.

- **Serbian Dining Etiquette:** Wait for the host to start eating, and keep your hands visible on the table. It's polite to finish everything on your plate.

6. Vegetarian and Dietary Preferences

If you have dietary preferences or restrictions, don't worry – the Danube River region offers options for every palate:

- **Vegetarian Options:** Many traditional dishes can be adapted to vegetarian versions. Be sure to communicate your preferences to restaurant staff.

- **Gluten-Free and Allergies:** While some traditional dishes may contain gluten or allergens, modern eateries and accommodations are often well-equipped to cater to dietary restrictions.

7. Embrace the Experience

The Danube River cruise is not just a culinary journey – it's an opportunity to immerse yourself in the flavors, traditions, and stories that define the region's cuisine. Be open to trying new dishes, engaging with locals to learn about their culinary heritage, and savoring every bite as you traverse the river's meandering path.

Reflection Message to Travelers:
Dear Travelers,

As your Danube River cruise comes to a close, take a moment to reflect on the incredible journey you've embarked upon. The picturesque landscapes, historic cities, and the bonds formed with fellow travelers have created a tapestry of memories that will forever be etched in your heart. From the enchanting streets of Vienna to the vibrant energy of Budapest, each destination has offered a unique glimpse into the rich cultures that line the river's banks.

As you bid farewell to the Danube's waters and the camaraderie you've shared with newfound friends, remember that the journey isn't just about the places you've visited. It's about the stories exchanged, the laughter shared, and the moments of awe that have expanded your horizons. Carry these experiences with you as you continue your life's journey, knowing that the Danube's beauty and the connections you've made will remain a source of inspiration.

May the memories of this adventure fill your days with joy, curiosity, and a deep appreciation for the diverse world we inhabit. As you return to your homes, remember that the spirit of the Danube will always be a part of you, reminding you that every ending is a new beginning, and every farewell is an opportunity to embrace the experiences that await.

With warm wishes and heartfelt reflections,

Made in the USA
Columbia, SC
11 January 2024

30310286R00054